I0822995

# WILD EMBROIDERY

# WILD EMBROIDERY

## 16 Botanical Designs Inspired by the Beauty of the Arts & Crafts Movement

NORIKO LIVINGSTONE

## Other Schiffer Craft Books on Related Subjects:

*Embroidery Garden: Artful Designs Inspired by Nature*, Yanase Rei, ISBN 978-0-7643-6424-2

*Vintage French Needlework: 300 Authentic Cross-Stitch Patterns–Flowers, Borders, and Alphabets from Antique Textiles*, Véronique Maillard, ISBN 978-0-7643-6764-9

*Arts and Crafts Embroidery*, Laura Euler, ISBN 978-0-7643-4409-1



Photographs by Noriko Livingstone unless otherwise credited.

Library of Congress Control Number: 2026932888



Designed by Lori Malkin Ehrlich
Cover design by Lindsay Hess
Type set in Ernestine Pro / Area Normal
Photo on facing page: Satoshi Nukui

ISBN: 978-0-7643-7242-1
Printed in China

10 9 8 7 6 5 4 3 2 1

Published by Schiffer Craft
An imprint of Schiffer Publishing, Ltd.
4880 Lower Valley Road
Atglen, PA 19310
Phone: (610) 593-1777; Fax: (610) 593-2002
Email: Info@schifferbooks.com
Web: www.schifferbooks.com

Beauty, which is what is meant by *art*, using the word
in its widest sense, is, I contend, no mere accident to human life,
which people can take or leave as they choose,
but a positive necessity of life . . .

–William Morris, Feb. 19, 1880

# CONTENTS

# INTRODUCTION

**AS AN EMBROIDERY DESIGNER**, I often get inspiration from nature and museum art. Why this mix? It's partly because I've visited natural places and museums many times with my mother and grandmother, ever since I was little. So, together with the physical beauty of the natural world and of the artwork, my memories developed a beloved layer of meaning for me.

My designs are often inspired by designs created in the seventeenth to nineteenth centuries. My ideal is beauty and use. I want to produce practical projects. It brings me pleasure when stitchers, like you, can use my designs in your daily life, with no need to put them away in a drawer after enjoying the stitching!

I lived in England to study one of my favorite arts, floristry. There I appreciated that people cherish beautiful things from long ago. Whether it was walking in the streets, visiting the museums, or enjoying those gardens, I gathered many ideas that eventually drew me closer to understanding the Arts and Crafts movement.

The Arts and Crafts movement started in Britain in the second half of the nineteenth century and spread to Europe, North America, and Japan. It was a reaction by certain artists and craftspeople to what they were noticing around them: the change in the quality of items and the quality of people's lives due to mass production and industrialization.

These makers who encouraged what later became known as the Arts and Crafts movement were passionate about holding on to principles such as handmaking, design simplicity, natural materials, and using beautiful things in everyday life.

The Arts and Crafts movement impacted the design and manufacturing methods of many items, from buildings to jewelry. Designs were often based on floral motifs, influenced by medieval or oriental patterns. A pioneer of the movement was William Morris, who was a British designer, writer, poet, and social activist; people continue to enjoy his designs today. This statement of his, relating to the Arts and Craft movement, is familiar: "Have nothing in your houses that you do not know to be useful or believe to be beautiful." Beauty and use was the aim.

May Morris also influenced the movement, especially through her expert embroidery. She was the younger of Morris's two daughters. She would eventually become a successful embroidery designer, jeweler, socialist, and editor. After studying embroidery at what is now the Royal College of Art, she became head of the embroidery department at Morris & Co. at the young age of twenty-three and is one of the most influential British embroidery artists.

The Arts and Crafts philosophy placed an emphasis on craftsmanship, simplicity, nature, and environmental-based inspiration. The movement encouraged the use of local, sustainable materials such as wood, stone, glass, and clay. Many producers, including Morris & Co., avoided industrially-produced chemical dyes and instead used fibers dyed with natural sources. The makers valued the connection between people and nature. The ideal was for finely crafted products to be available to all people, not only wealthy people. But high-quality handcraft was difficult to scale up to share with many people, and the philosophy later evolved to acceptance of machines for use in some aspects. The Arts and Crafts movement also varied depending on the era and the location.

I think we can change something that is based on another era's tradition to fit our own lifestyle, and that doing so is a natural way to inherit and keep the tradition.

We could also learn from the Arts and Crafts movement's environment-based inspiration in this era. We are producing convenient consumption, which has negative impacts on nature. When we buy a product, we could consider whether it's sustainable, recyclable, or eco-friendly, instead of just another convenient-to-consume thing.

I wondered how I could do that as a member of the crafts industry and chose to produce my book by using paper and cover material certified by the Forest Stewardship Council, which works to mitigate climate and biodiversity crises through sustainable forest management around the world. The paper materials certified by FSC are produced following their principles of zero deforestation, protection of plant and animal species, fair wages for forestry workers, and consulting with communities living in and around forests. My hope is that we'll begin to see more about the background and sourcing behind the craft products we buy, which gives us an opportunity to think about the environment.

Publishing a book also offers opportunities, and I dearly hope my book makes a social contribution. If you are inspired by my designs, and if they help you focus on nature, plants, and art around you, that to me is success. Take a break from the hustle and bustle of everyday life and enjoy some time to stitch and relax.

## A NOTE ON MATERIALS

The photographed projects were made with DMC size 25 cotton embroidery floss unless otherwise noted. This floss is certified Oeko-Tex® STANDARD 100, meeting the highest ecology standards. I used DMC needles numbers 6 through 8 for two or three strands, and needle number 5 for four to six strands. The 28-count linen fabric shown is often DMC.

Photo pages 12–13: Kohei Nukui

Wherever nature works,
there will be beauty.
–William Morris, "Art and the
Beauty of the Earth" (1881)

Simplicity of life,
begetting simplicity of taste,
that is, a love for sweet and
lofty things, is of all matters
most necessary for the
birth of the new and better
art we crave for; simplicity
everywhere, in the palace as
well as in the cottage.

–William Morris, Dec. 4, 1877

# INSPIRED by NATURE & GARDENS

**I GET A LOT OF INSPIRATION FROM NATURE** in its wild form, but also from being in gardens. I have often visited Bishop's Palace Gardens in Chichester, England, a public park that the city maintains, to sit on a bench and smell the plants' scents and feel the wind, not just look at the scenery. The garden is not too big, but it is in practically the heart of the historical part of the town and a very beautiful and comfortable place to visit. I really love the times I spend there.

I also arrange flowers, and for me floristry has some similarities to embroidery design. I enjoy thinking about texture, colors, space, and balance when I arrange flowers. When many kinds of unique "plant characters" work together well, I feel balanced, and as though you can actually see each element better and become more curious about each. That applies to my embroidery designs; those same feelings are important keys in creating them.

The Arts and Crafts artists also got many of their design inspirations from nature and gardens, crafting objects that reflected the design around them (and us) in nature. I hope you too feel a sense of comfort and familiarity from my designs.

# WILD MELODY

I created this design wishing for peace. As in nature, here many kinds of unique wildflowers live together, respecting each other, and the textures and colors make beautiful harmony. I hope that one day we can all live in peace. The flowers include a daffodil, violet, daisy, and forget-me-not.

**Level:** Intermediate

**Design's dimensions:**
4.92" (w) × 4.80" (h)
12.5 cm (w) × 12.2 cm (h)
**Floss colors:** See diagram
**Stitches used:** See diagram
**Hoop size:** 6" (15.5 cm)
**Cloth:** 28-count linen (Shown: DMC, color 842)

## WILD MELODY

### THREAD COLORS

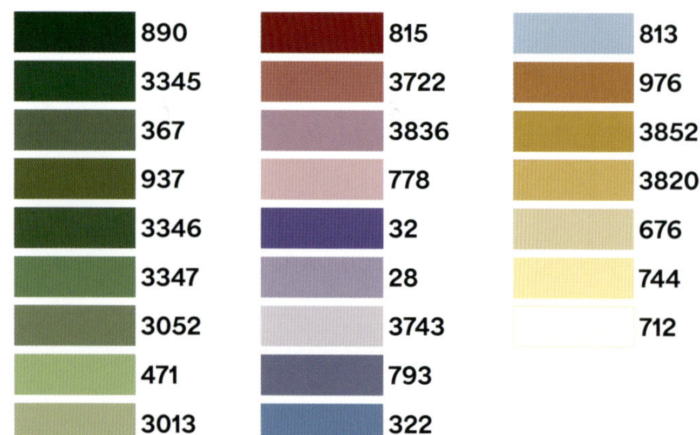

| | | |
|---|---|---|
| 890 | 815 | 813 |
| 3345 | 3722 | 976 |
| 367 | 3836 | 3852 |
| 937 | 778 | 3820 |
| 3346 | 32 | 676 |
| 3347 | 28 | 744 |
| 3052 | 3743 | 712 |
| 471 | 793 | |
| 3013 | 322 | |

### STITCHES

- **B** Back stitch
- **Ch** Chain stitch
- **F** Fishbone stitch
- **Fr** French knot
- **L** Long-and-short stitch
- **O** Outline stitch
- **S** Satin stitch
- **St** Straight stitch

All stitches are 3 strands.
French knot: Wind the thread around the needle 3 times.
Orange flower: Stitch Straight stitch using 676 on the 976 Long-and-short stitch.
F 937
S 3820
St 676: 2 each
L 712
Ch 3345
B 32
F 793
S 32
Fr 3820
O 3836
L 976
B 28
O 3347
Fr 28
S 28
Fr 744
Ch 3852
Fr 3743
S 3820
O 3345
F 3820
O 471
Ch 890
S 3346
F 890
F 3345
Fr 676
St 3052
S 813
Fr 712
F 367
Fr 3820
L 3722
O 471
St 3013
S 3013
O 3013
Fr 3820
O 3052
L 712
L 778
F 3722
St 3722
O 937
S 815
S 3345
O 3013
S 471
S 322
F 3347
Fr 3820
Fr 976
Fr 676
O 367
F 32
O 3346
L 28
F 890
L 676
St 3743
F 471
Pink flower: Stitch Straight stitch using 3722 on the 778 Long-and-short stitch.
Light purple violet: Stitch Straight stitch in different lengths using 3743 on the 28 Long-and-short stitch. The bottom petal is 3 stitches; the top petals are 2 stitches.

## ROBIN

This design features a robin, which I chose because they are familiar and loved by so many people in so many places. Mine is an English robin. You likely have your own local species of robin to enjoy! I used several kinds of stitches to give the embroidery some interesting movement. The abstract design of the eye and the plants around the bird were inspired by a grouping of jewelry I noticed one day.

**Level:** Intermediate

**Design's dimensions:**
4.72" (w) × 4.44" (h)
12 cm (w) × 11.3 cm (h)
**Floss colors:** See diagram
**Stitches used:** See diagram
**Hoop size:** 6" (15.5 cm)
**Cloth:** 28-count linen (Shown: DMC, color 3782)

## ROBIN

## THREAD COLORS

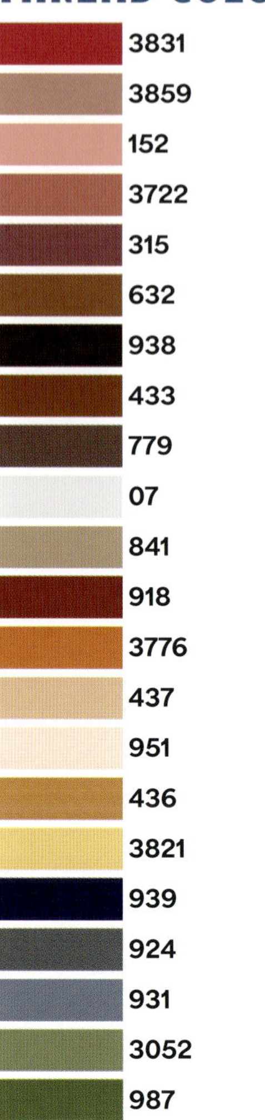


## STITCHES

- **Ch** Chain stitch
- **F** Fishbone stitch
- **Fr** French knot
- **L** Long-and-short stitch
- **O** Outline stitch
- **S** Satin stitch
- **St** Straight stitch

# ROBIN

Light blue flower:
Stitch Straight stitch using 951 on the 931 Long-and-short stitch.
All stitches are 2 strands except where stated as 3.
French knot: Wind the thread around the needle 3 times.
The eye:
Stitch Straight stitch using 437 on the 3776 Long-and-short stitch.
L 931
Fr 3821 - 3 strands
St 3821 - 3 strands
St 951
S 152
S 3831
S 939
St 437
S 924
O 938 - 3 strands
F 918
F 939
Ch 632
O 07
O 433 - 3 strands
L 841
L 3859
O 779
L 07
L 3776
F 987
O 433
F 3052
L 437
St 3859
L 951
L 436
L 3722
S 315
O 3859

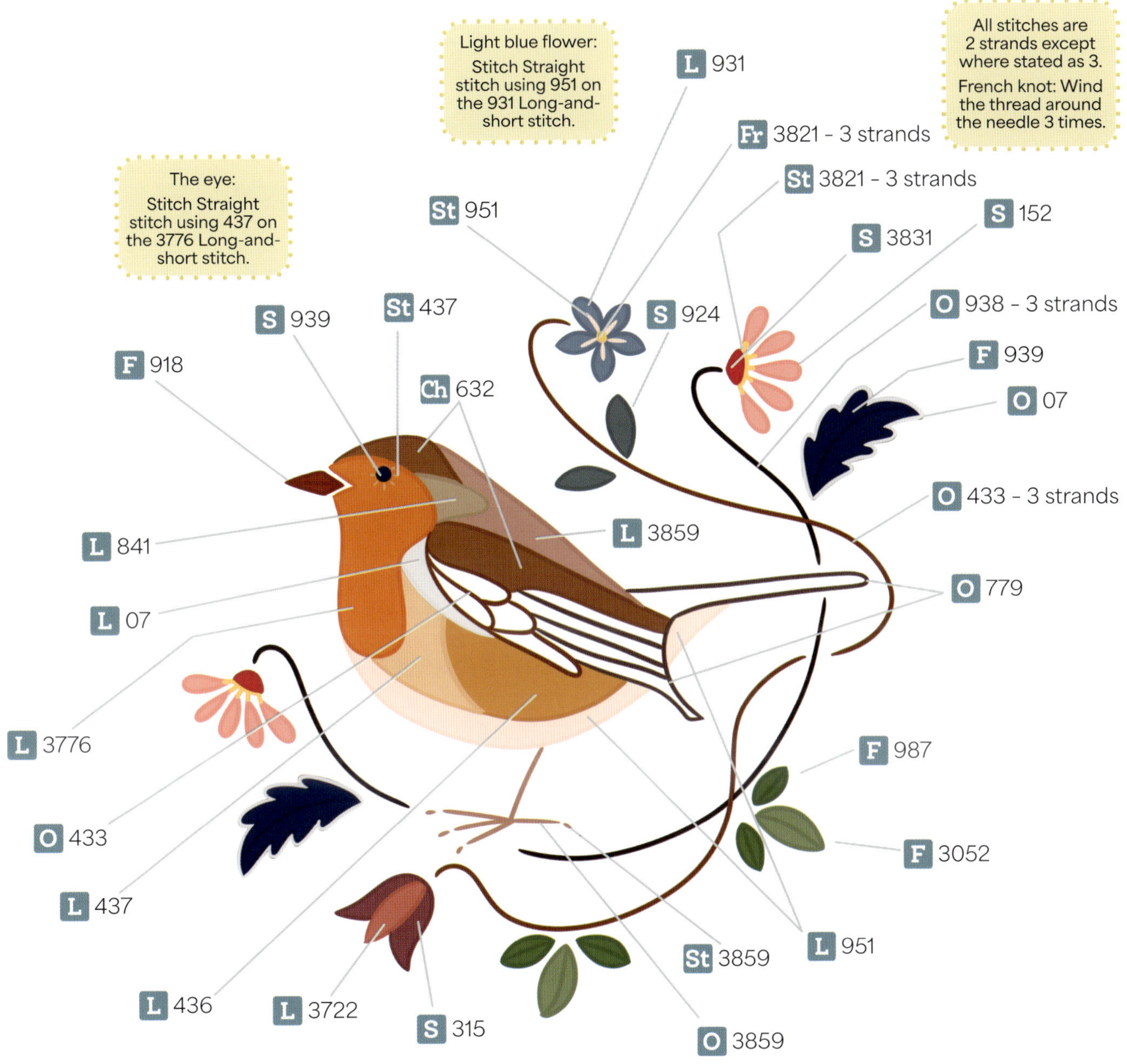

# ROSE & DAISY

If you are a beginner, this is a good design to start with. The results are elegant and well balanced. I created it as a dual-use shoulder bag / pouch. This design would also fit especially well on other types of bags and on aprons. I think it's nice to stitch on kids' garments too!

**Level:** Beginner

**Design's dimensions:**
8.27" (w) × 2.83" (h)
21 cm (w) × 7.2 cm (h)
Bag size: 8.27" (w) × 5.91" (h), gusset 1"
21 cm (w) × 15 cm (h), gusset 2.5 cm
**Floss colors:** See diagram
**Stitches used:** See diagram
**Cloth:** Linen (bag front and back)

# ROSE & DAISY

RIGHT: Back of bag

# ROSE & DAISY

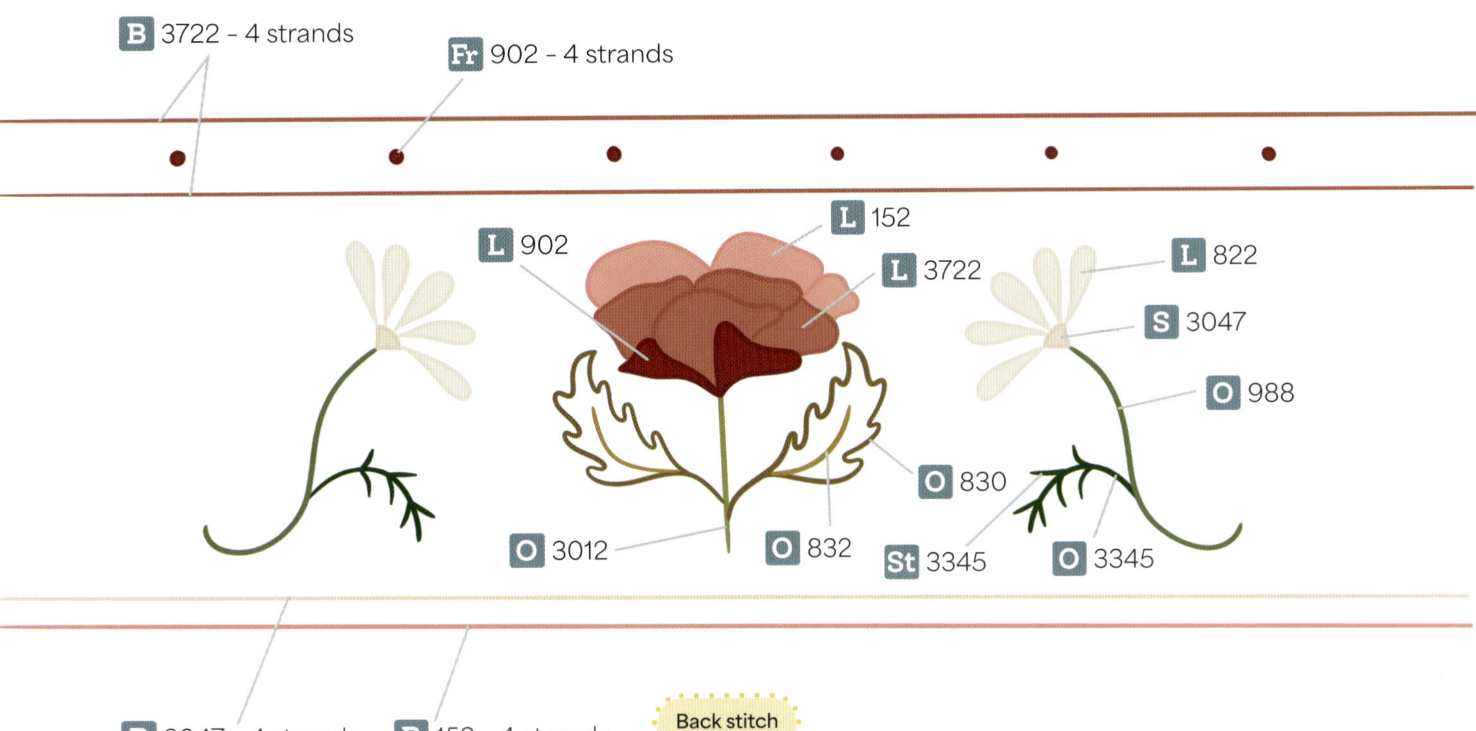


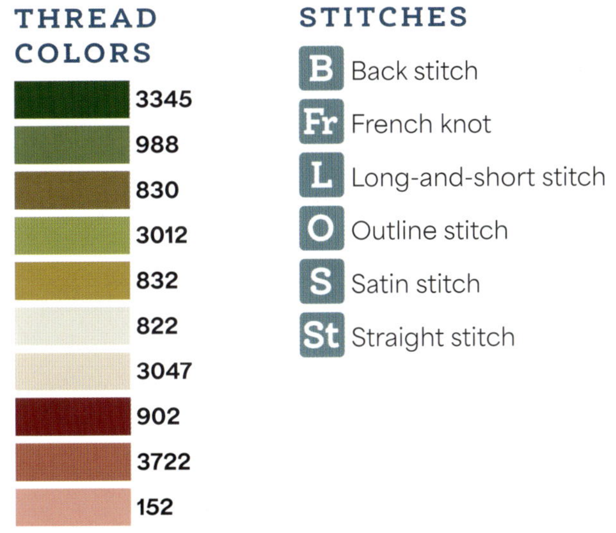

## THREAD COLORS

- 3345
- 988
- 830
- 3012
- 832
- 822
- 3047
- 902
- 3722
- 152

## STITCHES

- **B** Back stitch
- **Fr** French knot
- **L** Long-and-short stitch
- **O** Outline stitch
- **S** Satin stitch
- **St** Straight stitch

# CHESTNUT TIGER BUTTERFLY

I created this design with the thought of having it resemble a piece of jewelry. Chestnut tiger butterflies come to a mountain near my house in October, visiting from southwestern countries. I'm always excited to see this beautiful species each year, and the design here is a way to share that happy thrill with you.

**Level:** Beginner

**Design's dimensions:**
4.41" (w) × 2.48" (h)
11.2 cm (w) × 6.3 cm (h)
**Floss colors:** See diagram
**Stitches used:** See diagram
**Hoop size:** 5" (13 cm)
**Cloth:** Linen

# CHESTNUT TIGER BUTTERFLY

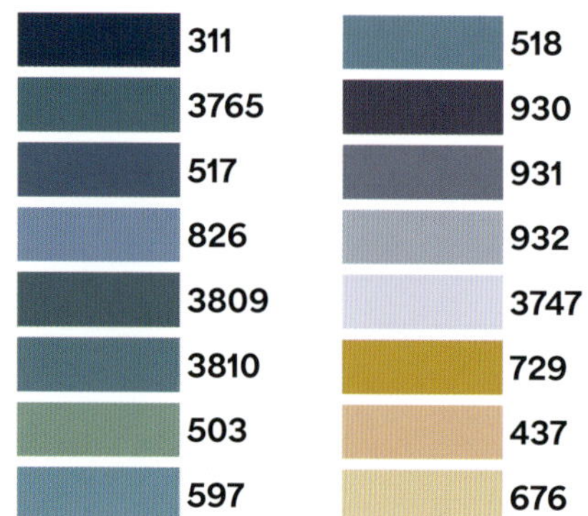


## STITCHES

- **Ch** Chain stitch
- **Fr** French knot
- **O** Outline stitch
- **S** Satin stitch

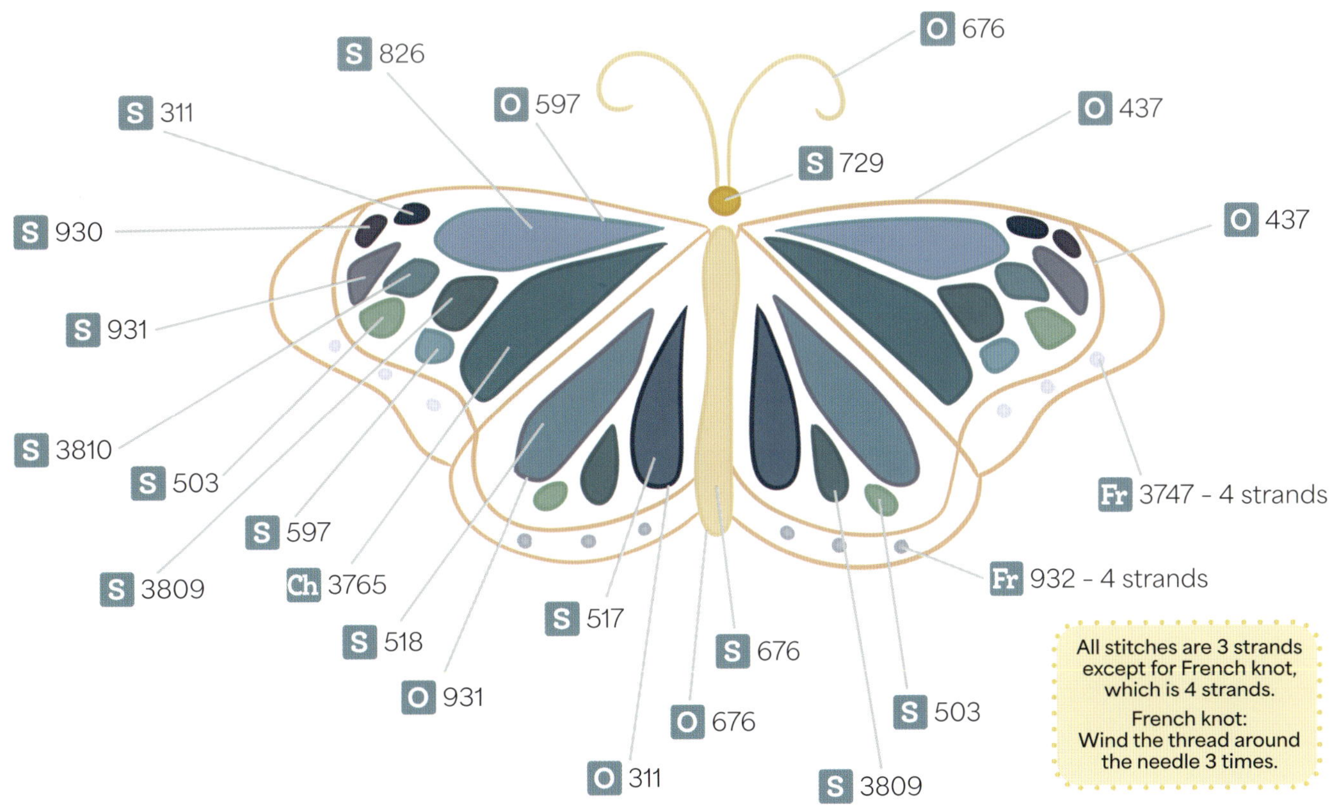
S 826
O 597
O 676
S 311
S 729
O 437
S 930
O 437
S 931
S 3810
S 503
S 597
S 3809
Ch 3765
S 518
O 931
S 517
S 676
O 676
O 311
S 3809
S 503
Fr 3747 - 4 strands
Fr 932 - 4 strands
All stitches are 3 strands except for French knot, which is 4 strands.
French knot: Wind the thread around the needle 3 times.

## SISTER RABBITS

This design isn't that complicated but is gorgeous to carry with you. Rabbits are yet another part of the natural world to appreciate. This design reminds me of the times I took the train from London to the south. Soon after the train left the city, we'd see rabbits and deer.

**Level:** Intermediate

**Design's dimensions:**
9.49" (w) × 5.16" (h)
24 cm (w) × 13.1 cm (h)
Bag size: 11.42" (w) × 7.48" (h), gusset 1.6"
29 cm (w) × 19 cm (h), gusset 4 cm

**Floss colors:** See diagram
**Stitches used:** See diagram
**Cloth:** Mixed fiber content

# SISTER RABBITS

All stitches are 3 strands except for the center of the white flower, which is 4 strands.

French knot:
Wind the thread around the needle 3 times

Fr 676 - 4 strands

O 904

L 3047

O 3347

St 3347

## STITCHES

- **B** Back stitch
- **F** Fishbone stitch
- **Fr** French knot
- **L** Long-and-short stitch
- **O** Outline stitch
- **S** Satin stitch
- **St** Straight stitch

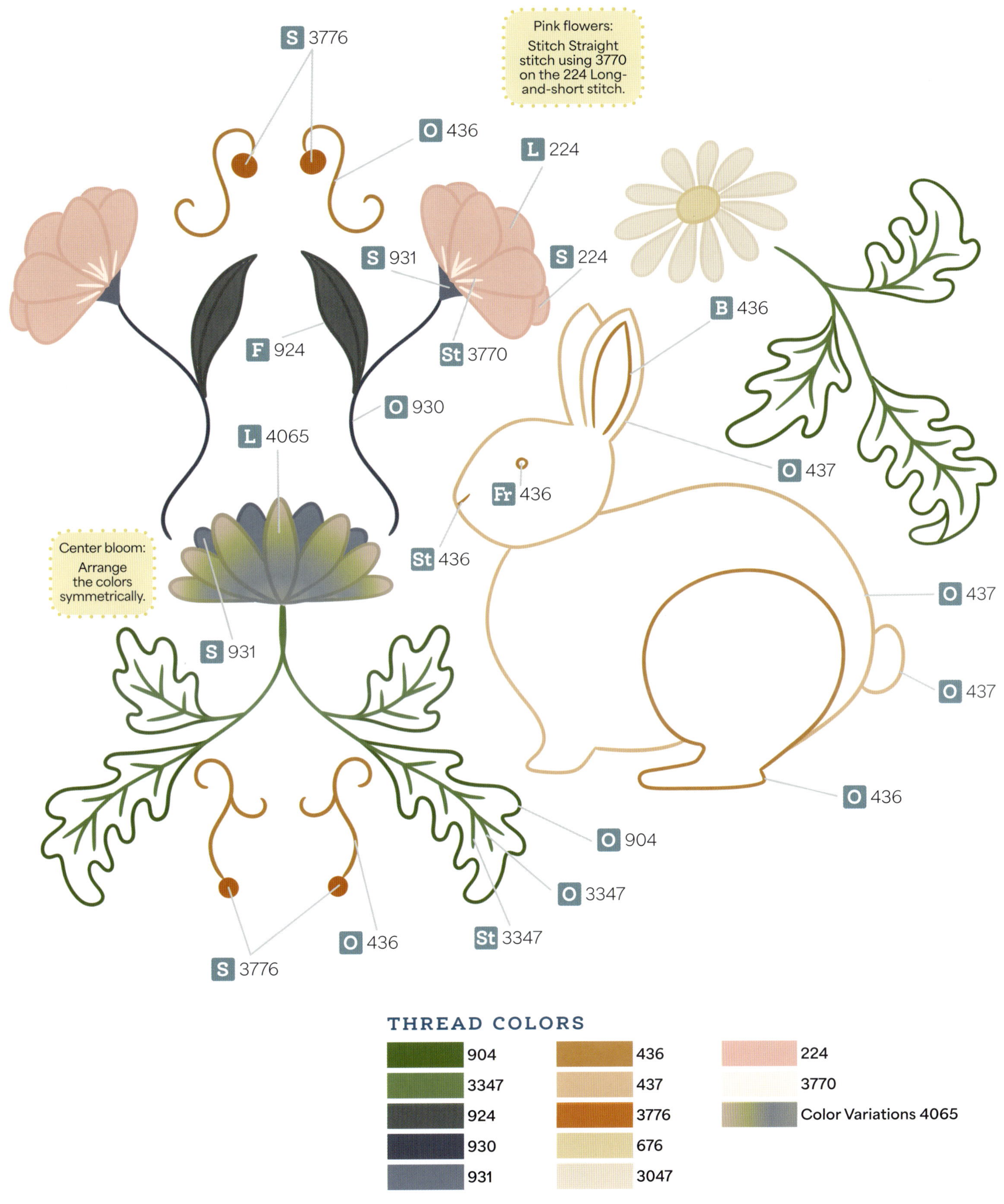
S 3776
Pink flowers:
Stitch Straight stitch using 3770 on the 224 Long-and-short stitch.
O 436
L 224
S 931
S 224
B 436
F 924
St 3770
O 930
L 4065
O 437
Fr 436
St 436
Center bloom:
Arrange the colors symmetrically.
O 437
S 931
O 437
O 436
O 904
O 3347
St 3347
O 436
S 3776
THREAD COLORS
904
3347
924
930
931
436
437
3776
676
3047
224
3770
Color Variations 4065

## BELLE

In the version of the tale "Beauty and the Beast" shown in the 2017 live-action film, there is a scene I love: a dance party in a castle in the eighteenth century, with beautiful flower arrangements and people wearing lovely embroidered costumes. It combines so many of my favorite things! For me, this design expresses that whirling mixture of beauty. I stitched it with a number 5 needle.

**Level:** Advanced

**Design's dimensions:**
21.85" (w) × 14.18" (h)
55.5 cm (w) × 36 cm (h)
Cloth: 24.02" (w) × 20" (h)
61 cm (w) × 50.8 cm (h)

**Floss colors:** See diagram
**Stitches used:** See diagram
**Cloth:** 28-count linen

## BELLE

Template shown at 70% of actual size

# BELLE

THREAD COLORS
822
739
3770
632
437
729
435
436
3045
3046
745
3822
3820
3856
977
905
3347
3012
734
3348
3013
930
931
3760
813
3841
3835
3836
316
3042
3743
154
315
223
3712
760
758
224
STITCHES
Ch Chain stitch
F Fishbone stitch
Fr French knot
L Long-and-short stitch
O Outline stitch
S Satin stitch
St Straight stitch
O 437
L 3046
Pale yellow flowers: Stitch Long-and-short stitch with 3347 on the 745 Fishbone stitch.
Fr 745 6 strands
L 3760
L 813
L 3841
F 745
L 3347
O 3348
S 3820
Light blue flowers: Stitch Long-and-short stitch using 3760 on the 813 Long-and-short stitch.
L 3347
L 758
L 3013
L 3770
L 977
L 745
L 745
L 3856
L 3822
L 3820
Bottom of the rose petals: Stitch Long-and-short stitch on the Long-and-short stitch.
All stitches are 4 strands except for the French knot, which is 6 strands.
French knot: Wind the thread around the needle 3 times.

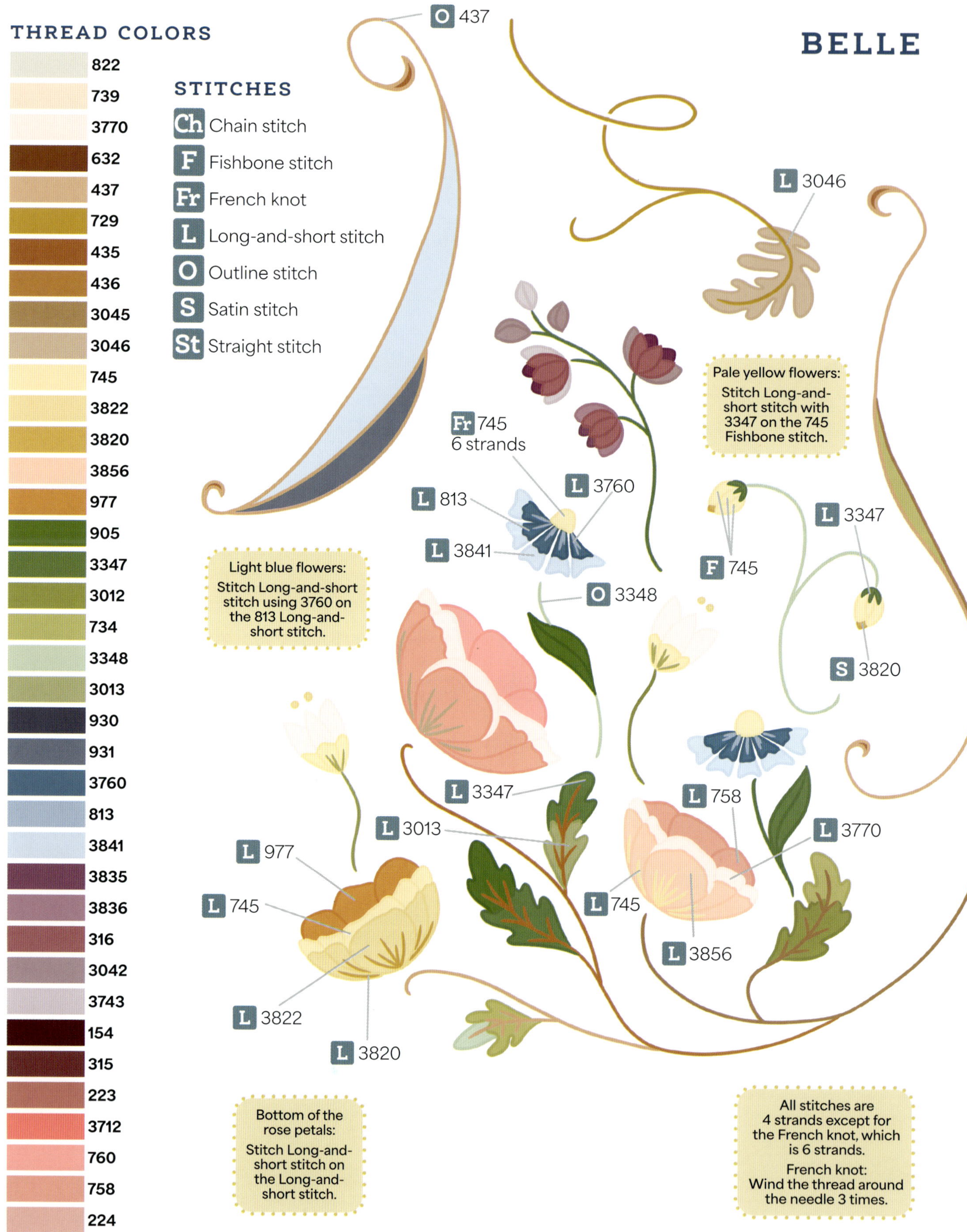

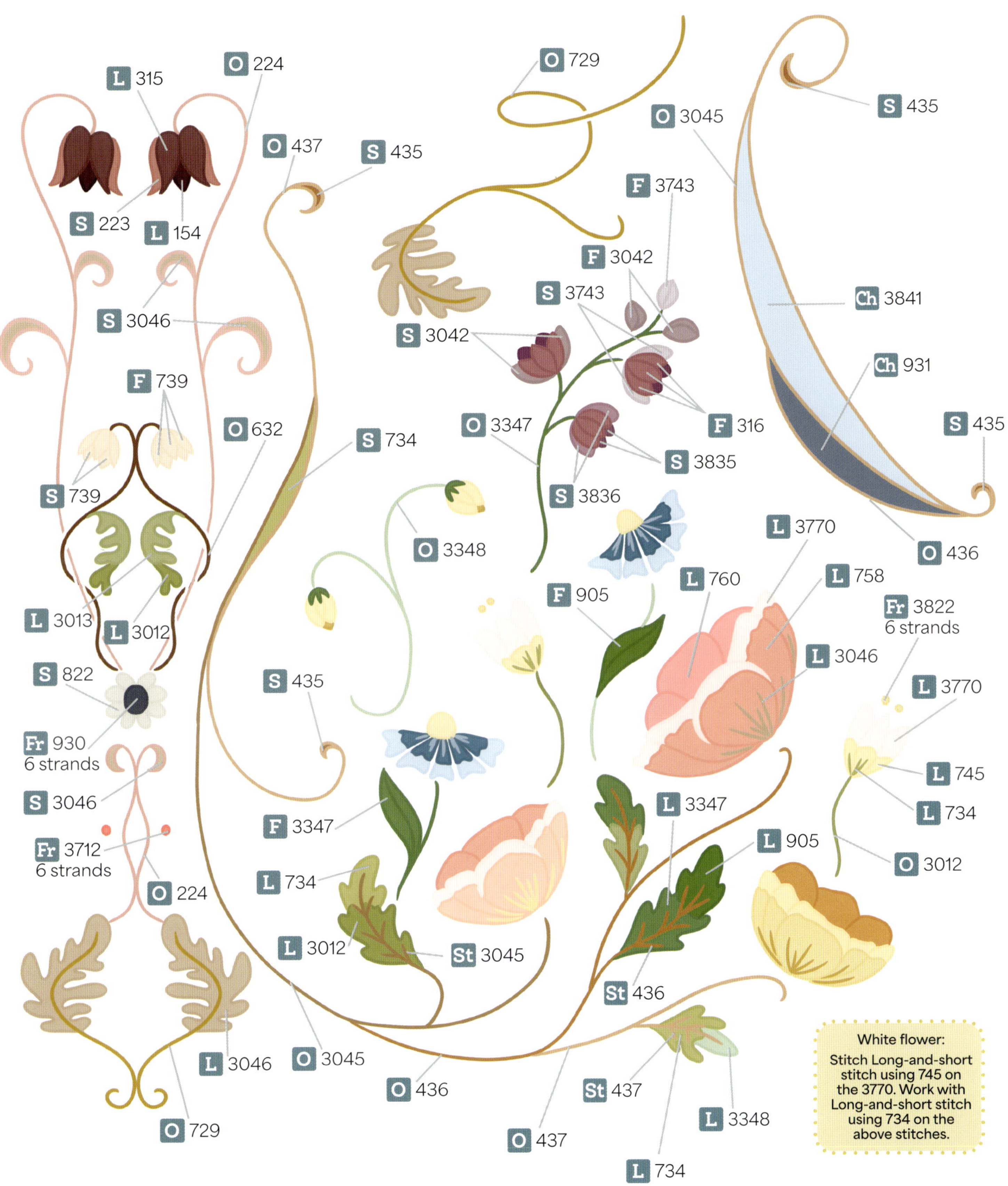


White flower:
Stitch Long-and-short stitch using 745 on the 3770. Work with Long-and-short stitch using 734 on the above stitches.

# INSPIRED by MUSEUMS

WORKS OF ART HAVE ALWAYS PLAYED A BIG ROLE in my design inspirations, so museums are dear to my heart. In its role of being a facility for art education and research, and to collect, preserve, and exhibit works of art, a museum bursts with traditions to learn from.

My designs clearly speak of older traditions but use them stylishly in a modern way. In my view, the best way to preserve a tradition is to be unafraid of changing some of its elements. Enjoy stitching them, and whenever you have the chance to visit these or any museums, enjoy deepening your knowledge!

The next two designs were created while I was feeling especially inspired by May Morris. The Morrises were so talented and worked in not one but various occupations as they made use of their extraordinary abilities, which they used to produce beautiful works that stand the test of time. If only I'd lived in that era and had been able to work with them. At least we have their complicated, graceful designs.

# MILLEFLEUR

My design came from a bedcover design made by May Morris for Mrs. Mary Grace Walker. Many years earlier, May and her mother, Jane, had created a bedcover design for May's own father, William Morris, at Kelmscott Manor, and this design is similar to it. Luckily for us today, Emery Walker Trust owns the bedcover, and we can admire it at Emery Walker's house in London.

**Level:** Beginner

**Design's dimensions:**
4.61" (w) × 4.92" (h)
11.7 cm (w) × 12.5 cm (h)
**Floss colors:** See diagram
**Stitches used:** See diagram
**Hoop size:** 6" (15.5 cm)
**Cloth:** 28-count linen

# MILLEFLEUR

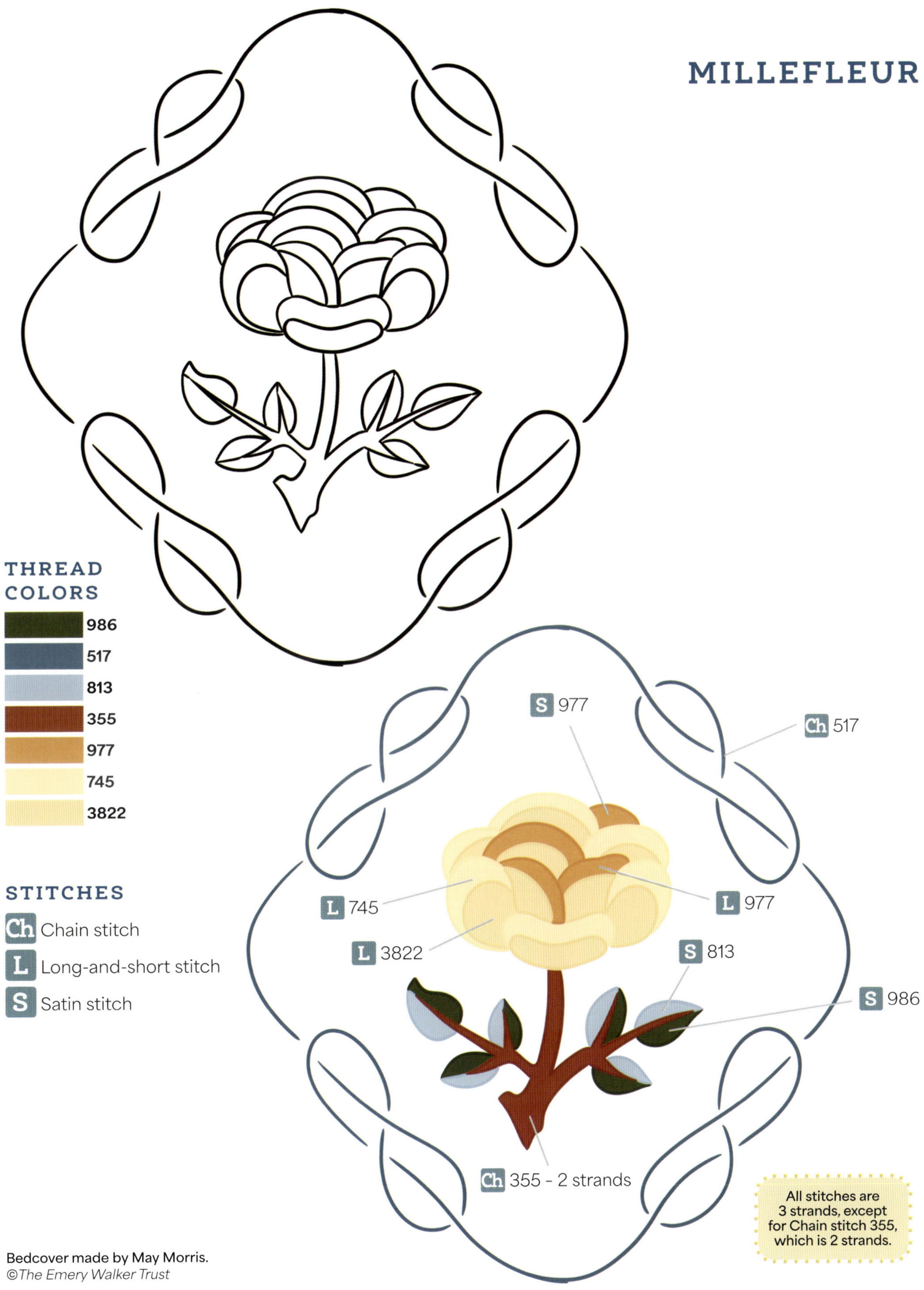


Bedcover made by May Morris.

BOTANIQUE
T.8.N°.75
Botanique.
DICT. UNIV. D'HIST. NAT.

## BIRD

My design was inspired by a set of bird hangings designed by William Morris. Emery Walker Trust owns them, and I instantly adored the color of the bird from the first time I saw it. I used an element of the Morris bird design and some flowers from it, with various kinds of stitches to keep this project interesting to embroider!

**Level:** Intermediate

**Design's dimensions:**
3.74" (w) × 3.94" (h)
9.5 cm (w) × 10 cm (h)
**Floss colors:** See diagram
**Stitches used:** See diagram
**Hoop size:** 6" (15.5 cm)
**Cloth:** 28-count linen

Bird hanging designed by William Morris, 1878, *detail.*
*Collection of The Metropolitan Museum of Art , Purchase, Edward C. Moore Jr. Gift, 1923*

## BIRD

S 3053

All stitches are 2 strands.

O 3363

S 334

Ch 3772

P 334

F 3857

S 3363

S 823

F 931

L 3857

S ECRU

Ch 3857

S 3859

F 3363

Ch 3859

L 739

O 3857

Ch 739

O 3859

Ch 3857

S 3363

S 3776

O 838

Ch 3859

Ch 3363

S ECRU

S 676

S 3776

S 3821

St 3821

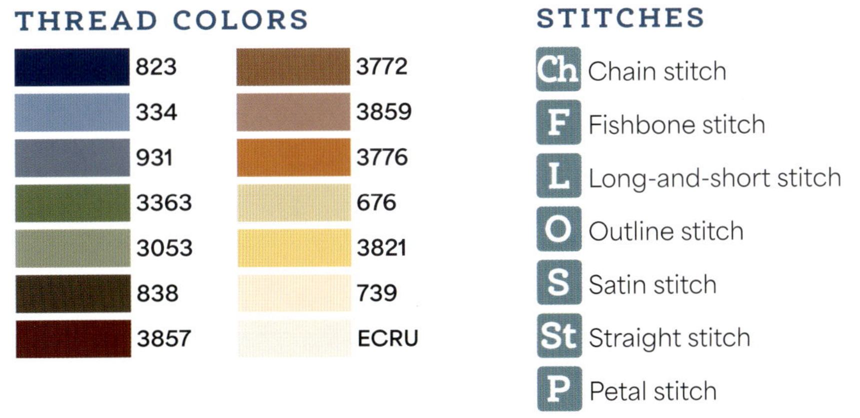

## HUMMINGBIRDS

The color combination that inspires this design is from a bowl created by Lucie Rie, an Austrian-born British studio potter. The bowl is pink porcelain with turquoise, white, and bronze colors. Its pretty, delicate, and down-to-earth design is expressed well, I think, by hummingbirds. My design features two birds drinking some of their favorite flowers' nectar: petunias, honeysuckle, and trumpet flowers.

**Level:** Advanced

**Design's dimensions:**
11.89" (w) × 8.46" (h)
30.2 cm (w) × 21.5 cm (h)
Cloth: 19.69" square
50 cm square
**Floss colors:** See diagram
**Stitches used:** See diagram
**Cloth:** Cotton-linen blend

## HUMMINGBIRDS

# HUMMINGBIRDS

## THREAD COLORS

- 223
- 224
- 372
- 435
- 502
- 503
- 320
- Anchor 1042
- Color Variations 4045
- 739
- 746
- 782
- 801
- 06
- 819
- 823
- 938
- 975
- 3046
- 3371
- 315
- 3821
- 3852
- 3863
- 3864
- 822

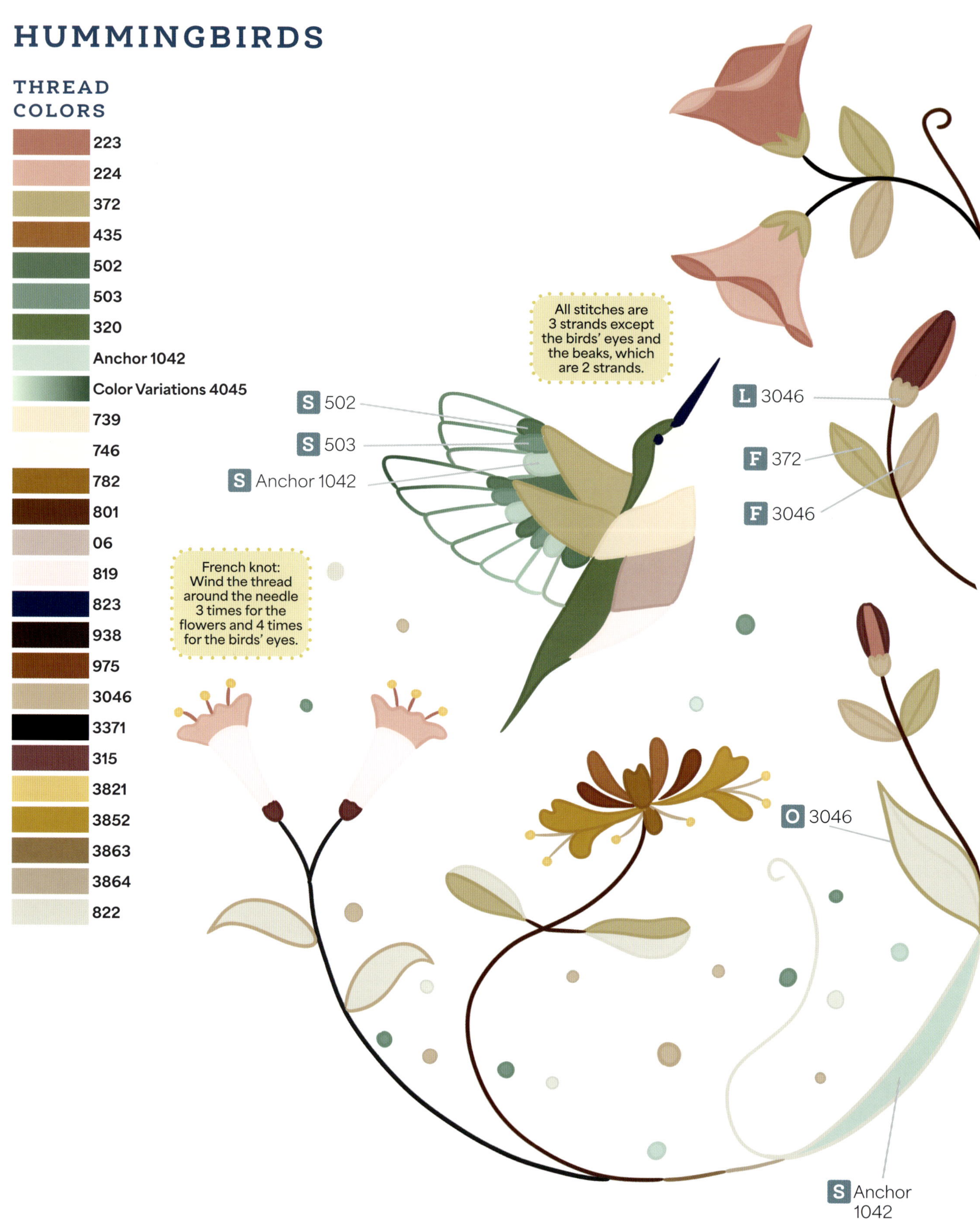

STITCHES
Ch Chain stitch
F Fishbone stitch
Fr French knot
L Long-and-short stitch
O Outline stitch
S Satin stitch
St Straight stitch
L 223
F 372
O 801
O 3371
S 224
S Anchor 1042
L 223
L 372
L 3046
O 938
F 3046
S 223
L 223
L 315
L 372
L 224
O 823 - 2 strands
Fr 823 - 2 strands, 4 loops
Ch 320
O 3046
S 372
L 746
L 739
L 06
L 819
S 822
O 938
S 503
O 801
L 315
O CV 4045
L 223
Ch 320
Fr 3821
F 372
St 223
L 782
L 224
F 3046
L 435
L 819
L 975
O 938
Fr 3821
S 315
F 822
S 822
L 3852
S 502
O 3046
O 3371
O 801
S 372
O 372
S 822
O 3046
S 3046
O 938
O 822
S 503
O 3864
O 3863
S Anchor 1042

## MARGUERITE DAISY

I created these baby shoes for my one-year-old daughter. The design was inspired by a pair of Manchu woman's shoes that are in the collection of the Brooklyn Museum. The colors are calm and soothing. I wanted to produce baby shoes with a detailed design and a simple fit: a unique way to offer some everyday beauty.

**Level:** Advanced

**Design's dimensions:**
5.95" (w) × 4.09" (h)
15.1 cm (w) × 10.4 cm (h)
Cloth: 7.87" (w) × 7.09" (h)
20 cm (w) × 18 cm (h)
Shoe length: 5.12" | 13 cm
**Floss colors:** See diagram
**Stitches used:** See diagram
**Cloth:** Mixed fiber content

Model: Emma

## MARGUERITE DAISY

# MARGUERITE DAISY

### THREAD COLORS

| | |
|---|---|
| 580 | 356 |
| 730 | 3712 |
| 830 | 758 |
| 831 | 436 |
| 370 | 676 |
| 734 | 945 |
| 632 | 926 |
| 3772 | 524 |
| 3722 | |

### STITCHES

- **Ch** Chain stitch
- **F** Fishbone stitch
- **Fr** French knot
- **L** Long-and-short stitch
- **O** Outline stitch
- **S** Satin stitch

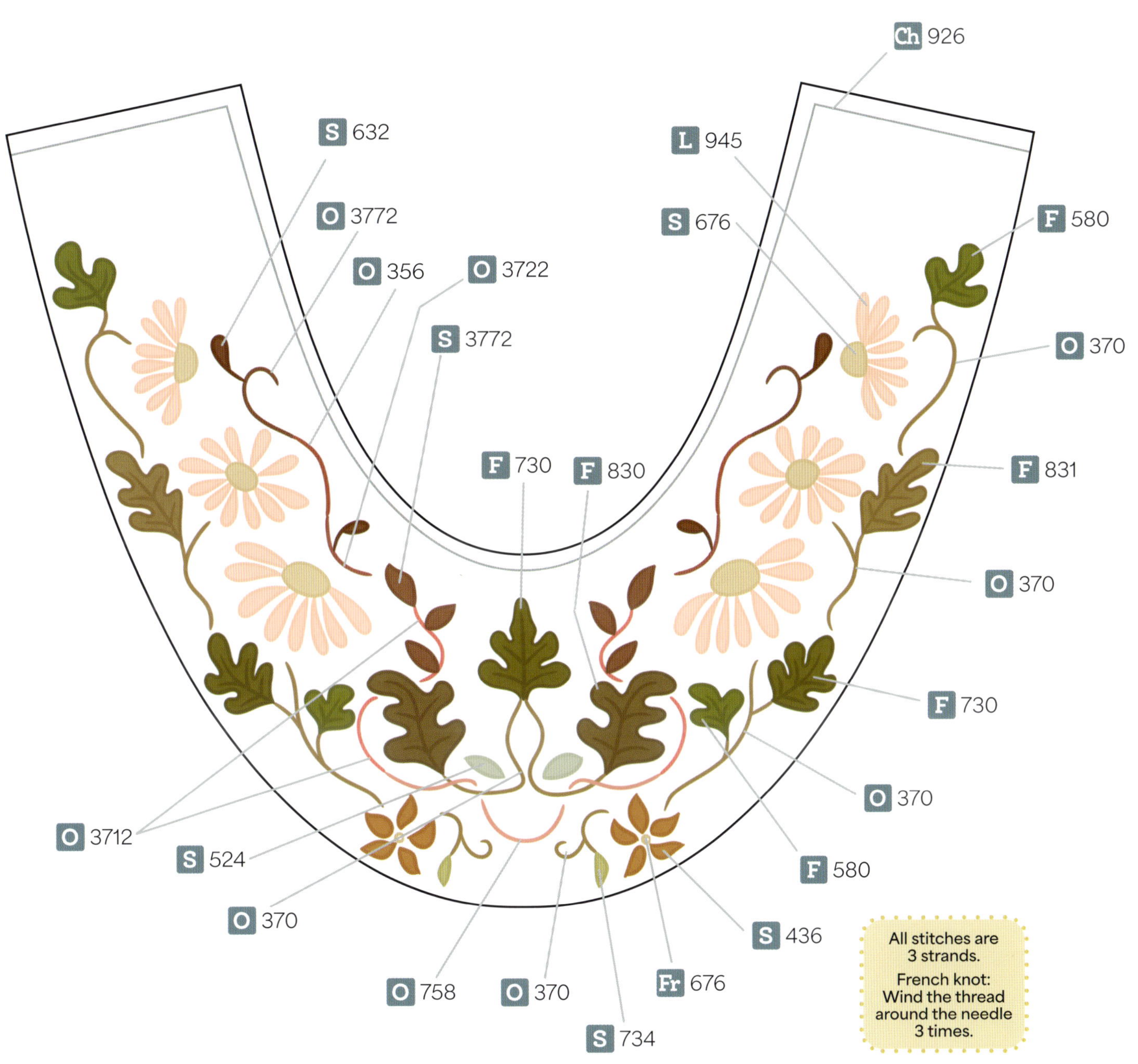
Ch 926
S 632
L 945
O 3772
S 676
F 580
O 356
O 3722
S 3772
O 370
F 730
F 830
F 831
O 370
F 730
O 370
O 3712
S 524
F 580
O 370
S 436
O 758
O 370
Fr 676
S 734
All stitches are 3 strands.
French knot: Wind the thread around the needle 3 times.

# TULIP SANCTUARY

This is inspired by embroidered and tasseled pouches made in the 1600s through the 1800s. It's a lovely design to carry with you on a modern pouch. The spring flowers—honeysuckle and violets along with the tulips—are gracefully in full bloom. No doubt your bag will be the center of attention! Stitch the design on an already-made pouch, or make your own as our ancestors would have.

**Level:** Intermediate

**Design's dimensions:**
6.46" (w) × 6.10" (h)
16.4 cm (w) × 15.5 cm (h)
Pouch size: 7.28" (w) × 8.66" (h) without tassel
18.5 cm (w) × 22 cm (h) without tassel
**Floss colors:** See diagram
**Stitches used:** See diagram
**Cloth:** Cotton, cupro, ribbon, tassel of DMC 799

## TULIP SANCTUARY

## THREAD COLORS

## STITCHES

- **Fr** French knot
- **L** Long-and-short stitch
- **O** Outline stitch
- **S** Satin stitch

# TULIP SANCTUARY

All stitches are 3 strands.
French knot: Wind the thread around the needle 3 times.

# OFFSHOOT

This dress for my eight-year-old daughter was inspired by a British waistcoat made in the seventeenth century with a design that is stitched in linen, silk, and metallic threads and is gorgeous. The Metropolitan Museum of Art holds this waistcoat. The creatures on the waistcoat show extreme detail of a scientific nature but are constructed with traditional continuous curves. So that everyone can enjoy my design, I created it for beginner level. I stitched it on a dress of my own design. You could also use it on a T-shirt, a blouse, or any item you'd like to make more beautiful.

**Level:** Beginner

**Design's dimensions:**
9.06" (w) × 4.33" (h)
23 cm (w) × 11 cm (h)
**Floss colors:** See diagram
**Stitches used:** See diagram
**Cloth:** Cotton blend

Waistcoat, British. *Collection of the Metropolitan Museum of Art*

Model: Mei

OFFSHOOT
Size this template to fit
your garment's neckline.

# OFFSHOOT

All stitches are 3 strands.
French knot: Wind the thread around the needle 3 times.
Fr 931
L 3752
F 937
S 939
L 3722
L 815
Fr 725
L 937
L 3771
L 734
F 3347
S 890
O 831

THREAD COLORS
890
937
3347
734
831
725
939
931
3752
815
3722
3771
STITCHES
F Fishbone stitch
Fr French knot
L Long-and-short stitch
O Outline stitch
S Satin stitch

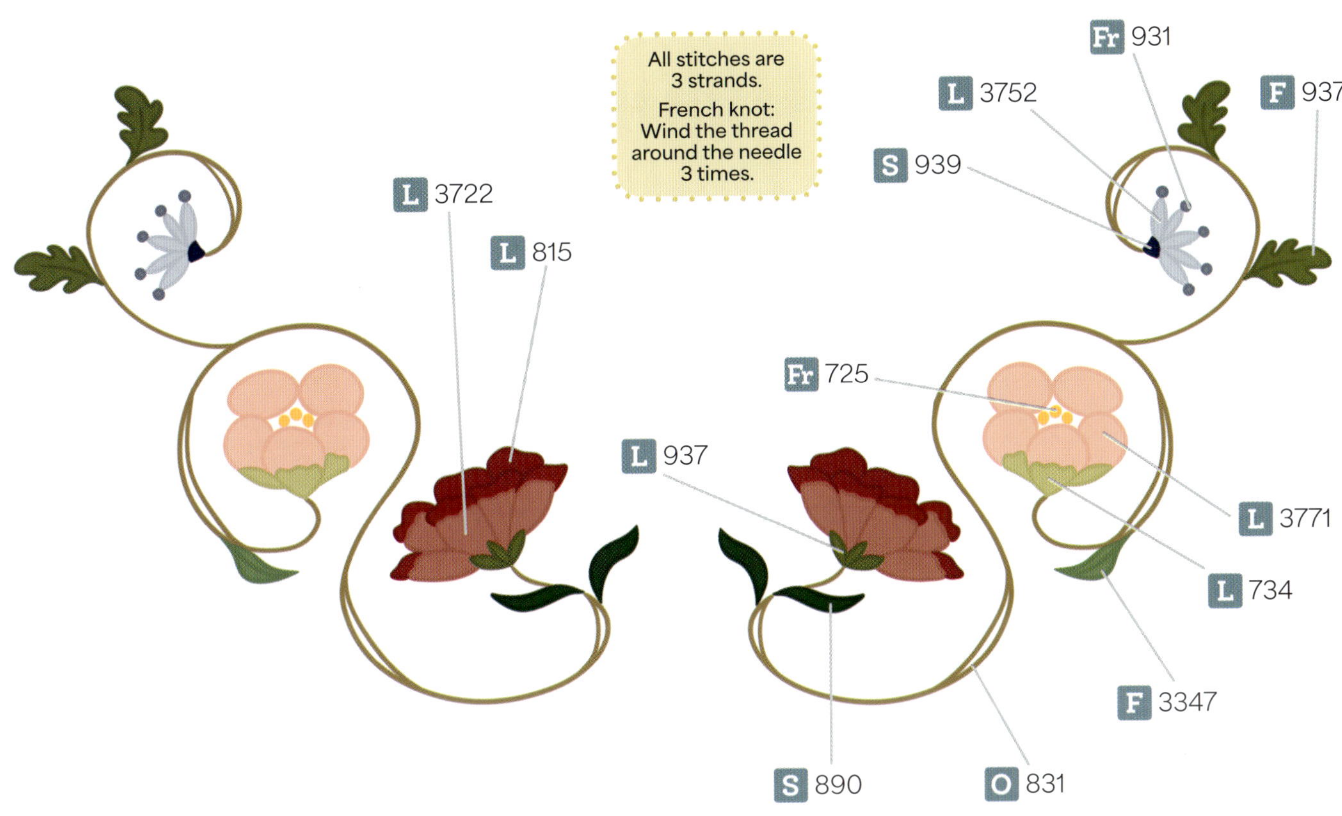

And yet here was Matthew
ernoon of a busy day, placi driving over the hollow and up
hill; moreover, he wore a hite collar and his best suit of
s, which was plain proof
had the buggy
ing a considera
and why w
en any other man i
nd that together,
questions. But Ma
omething pressing
hyest man alive a
place where
Cuthbert, at half-past three on the
going out of Avonlea;
which betokened that
here was Matthew Cuth-
Avonlea, Mrs. Rachel, deftly
ght have given a pretty good
ew so rarely went from home
d unusual which w

# INSPIRED by ALPINE NATURE

AS YOU ENJOY STITCHING THE BEAUTY of these alpine plants and ptarmigan, I would be happy if it also became an opportunity for you to understand more about the current alpine environment.

Due to global warming, there is less snowfall, a shorter snow season, and drier conditions, which means that alpine plants are being outcompeted by other plants, reducing their numbers. In addition, animals not previously found in high mountains are expanding their habitats there and causing damage. Some flower fields have already disappeared due to overgrazing damage by deer.

Many businesses related to outdoor activities are making efforts to protect the environment by producing their products ethically, since their work and their customers depend very obviously on nature. I think we can make that shift in the craft world too, where we are also closely connected to nature. Craft started by hand, using natural materials. Together we could align craft businesses toward more sustainable product sourcing and material choices, even as we still also use modern technology. Small ideas or actions might change the world if they are attractive and worth trying; the Arts and Crafts movement gives us a perfect example.

*Alpine plants* is a general term for plants that grow in the alpine zone, which is higher than the treeline (the limit at which tall trees can grow), but in a broader sense it includes not only alpine plants but also plants that grow in the subalpine zone. I apply the latter definition with these designs.

ALPINUS FLORA

## ALPINUS FLORA

This bird is based on the ptarmigan. They are famous in the high mountains in Japan; it's said that if you meet a ptarmigan, good things will happen and good fortune will come to you. They have long been cherished as divine birds. The beige flowers are Aleutian avens, and the pink and yellow flowers are komakusa, both of which are "alpinus flora": alpine plants. I stitched this with a number 5 needle.

**Level:** Advanced

**Design's dimensions:**
13.86" (w) × 13.98" (h)
35.2 cm (w) × 35.5 cm (h)
Cushion size: 16.73" dia.
42.5 cm dia.
**Floss colors:** See diagram
**Stitches used:** See diagram
**Cloth:** Cotton-linen blend

## ALPINUS FLORA

ALPINU

Template shown at
70% of actual size

S FLORA

Photo: Kohei Nukui

FLORA

## ALPINUS FLORA

All stitches are 4 strands except the French knot, which is 6 strands.

French knot: Wind the thread around the needle 3 times.

## THREAD COLORS

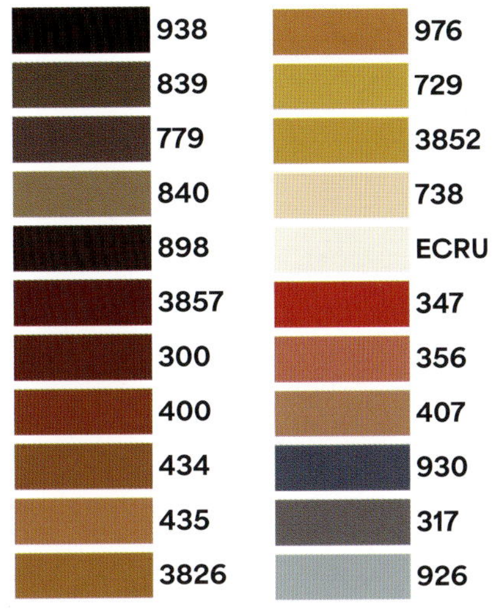

| | |
|---|---|
| 938 | 976 |
| 839 | 729 |
| 779 | 3852 |
| 840 | 738 |
| 898 | ECRU |
| 3857 | 347 |
| 300 | 356 |
| 400 | 407 |
| 434 | 930 |
| 435 | 317 |
| 3826 | 926 |

## STITCHES

- **B** Back stitch
- **Ch** Chain stitch
- **F** Fishbone stitch
- **Fr** French knot
- **L** Long-and-short stitch
- **O** Outline stitch
- **S** Satin stitch

Photo: Kohei Nukui

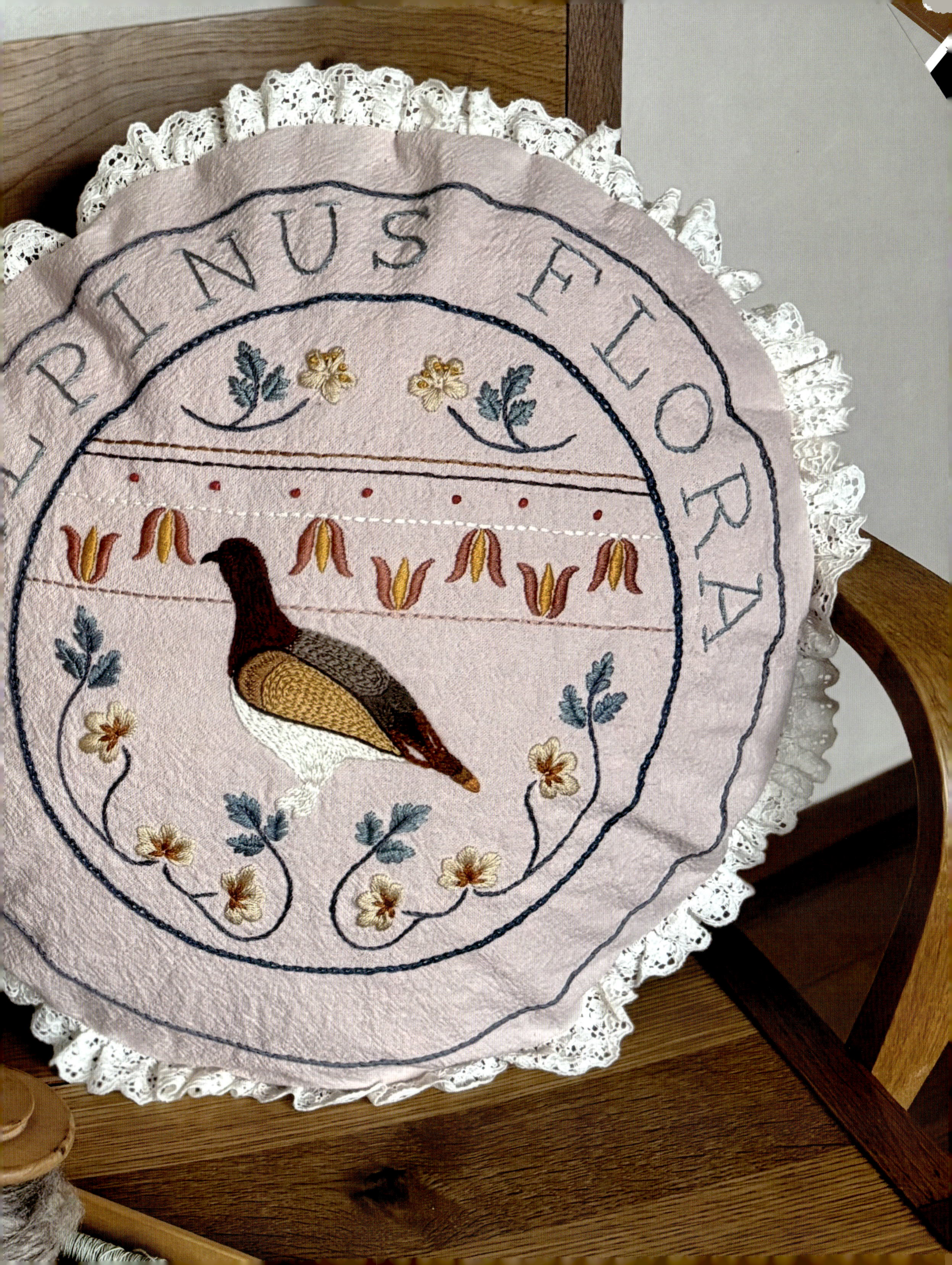
PINUS FLORA

Nicaragua

# HIMALAYAN BLUE POPPY

The Himalayan blue poppy is officially called *Meconopsis grandis*, and it grows at altitudes of roughly 9,800–16,400 feet (3,000–5,000 meters). It is native to the Himalayas and southwestern China. The wild species is very difficult to grow outside its home area. I like the fact that, no matter where you live, you can stitch it to enjoy its beauty.

**Level:** Beginner

**Design's dimensions:**
2.68" (w) × 3.43" (h)
6.8 cm (w) × 8.7 cm (h)
**Floss colors:** See diagram
**Stitches used:** See diagram
**Hoop size:** Oval, 5" × 7"
13.8 cm × 18.2 cm
**Cloth:** 28-count linen

# HIMALAYAN BLUE POPPY

## STITCHES

Ch Chain stitch
F Fishbone stitch
Fr French knot
L Long-and-short stitch
O Outline stitch
S Satin stitch
St Straight stitch

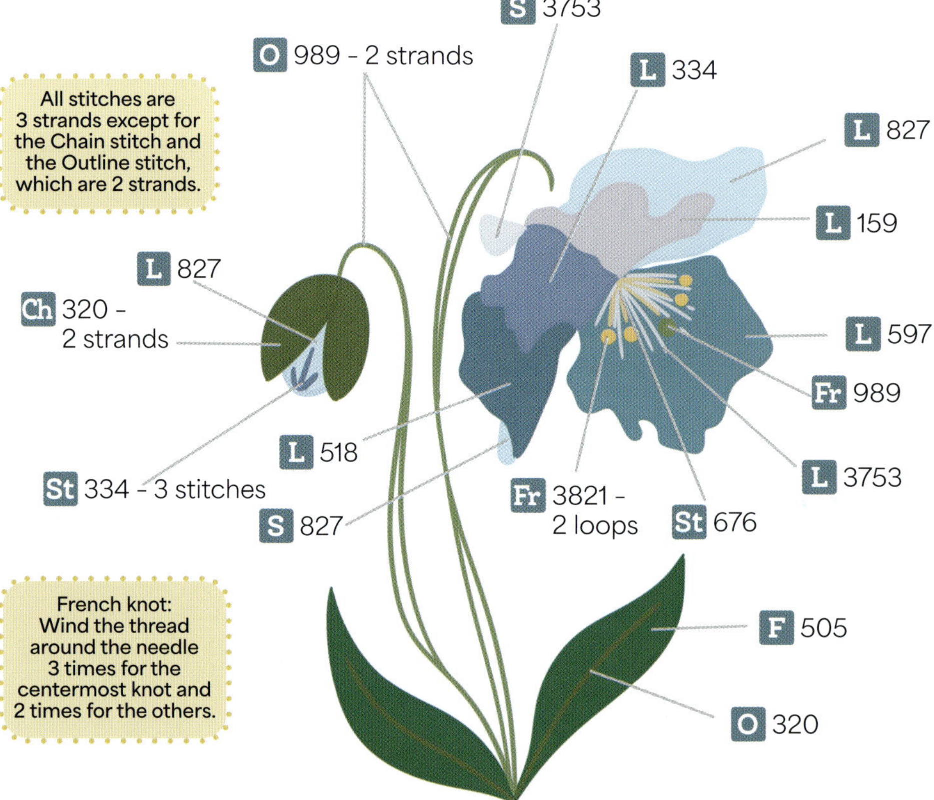

## SCABIOUS

Although scabious look fragile and very delicate, I have seen them blooming happily in strong winds in high mountain terrain. When we see scabious in its cultivated hybrid versions at the florist's, it is hard to imagine how the native species lives in such a tough environment. Stitching them can help us appreciate the contrast between their pretty appearance and their rugged durability.

**Level:** Beginner

**Design's dimensions:**
2.68" (w) × 3.43" (h)
6.8 cm (w) × 8.7 cm (h)
**Floss colors:** See diagram
**Stitches used:** See diagram
**Hoop size:** Oval, 5" × 7"
13.8 cm × 18.2 cm
**Cloth:** 28-count linen

# SCABIOUS

All stitches are 3 strands except for the French knot, which is 6 strands.
French knot: Wind the thread around the needle 3 times.

## KOMAKUSA

In Japan, komakusa is called the queen of alpine plants. While the flowers are beautiful, they grow on sand and gravel in high mountains, heavily eroded due to rain, wind, and snow: an extremely inhospitable environment for plants to grow in. The name, assigned to it by the famous Japanese botanist Tomitaro Makino, is based on the shape of the flower, resembling a horse's face: In kanji, *koma* means horse and *kusa* means grass.

**Level:** Beginner

**Design's dimensions:**
3.39" (w) × 3.82" (h)
8.6 cm (w) × 9.7cm (h)
**Floss colors:** See diagram
**Stitches used:** See diagram
**Hoop size:** Oval, 5" × 7"
13.8 cm × 18.2 cm
**Cloth:** 28-count linen

## KOMAKUSA

### THREAD COLORS

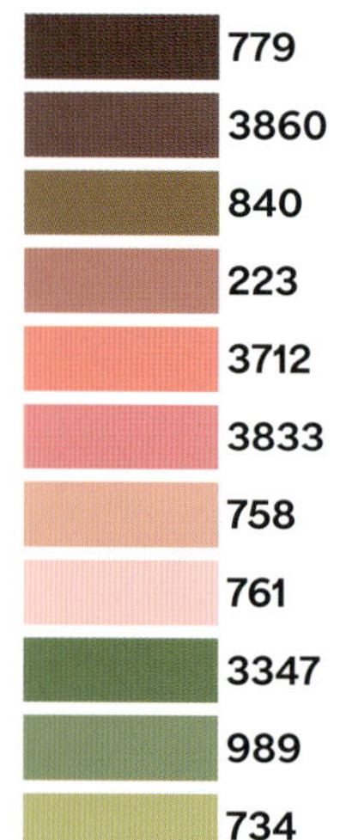


### STITCHES

- **B** Back stitch
- **F** Fishbone stitch
- **O** Outline stitch
- **S** Satin stitch
- **St** Straight stitch

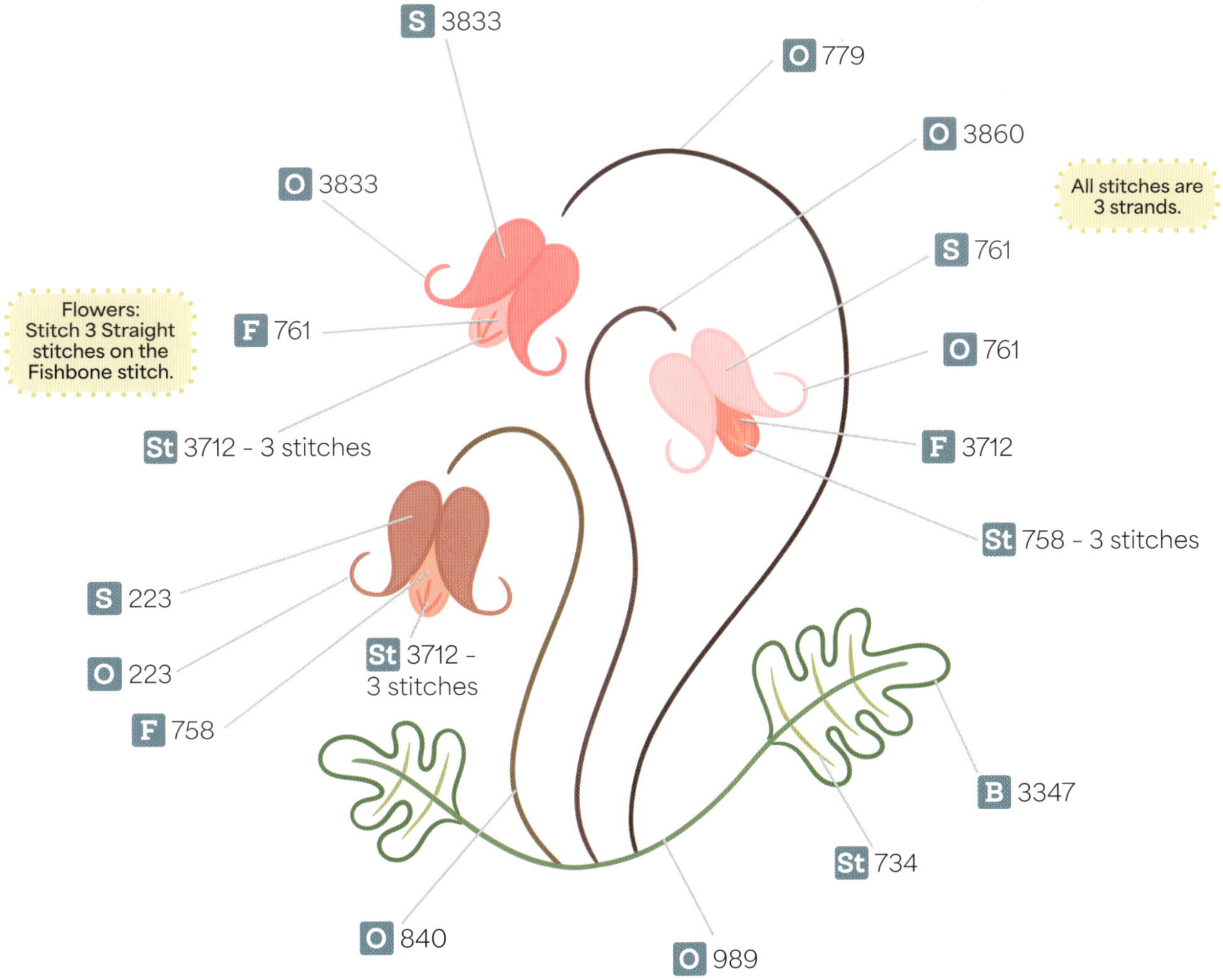

S 3833
O 779
O 3860
O 3833
All stitches are 3 strands.
S 761
Flowers: Stitch 3 Straight stitches on the Fishbone stitch.
F 761
O 761
St 3712 - 3 stitches
F 3712
St 758 - 3 stitches
S 223
O 223
St 3712 - 3 stitches
F 758
B 3347
St 734
O 840
O 989

# ACKNOWLEDGMENTS

With heartfelt gratitude to:

### THE ENTIRE TEAM AT SCHIFFER CRAFT

My sincere thanks for kindly giving me an opportunity and for all of your hard work. I am so honored to work with your team, which was a positive experience throughout. This book turned out to be much more wonderful than I had imagined. I cannot thank you enough!

### INSPIRATIONS STUDIOS

Your advice has helped me get this far, and I will always be grateful. Thank you so very much for including me in your beautiful publications.

### MY FAMILY

I am forever grateful for your warm support. I could not have produced this book without you all, which has made this book more special.

### MY FRIENDS

Thank you for caring about me as you always do; your encouragement means a lot to me.

I also would like to sincerely thank:

DMC
Polly Leonard at Selvedge
Helen Elletson at Emery Walker's House
The Metropolitan Museum of Art

**NORIKO LIVINGSTONE** is an acclaimed embroidery designer with a long-term love of the Arts and Crafts needlework aesthetic. She brings its timeless simplicity and natural beauty into her modern designs, aiming to help people appreciate nature and eco-sustainability. She has been featured by Inspirations Studios, Selvedge, and others and she is a brand sponsor for DMC.

Noriko also holds a degree in fashion art, is qualified as a curator, and is a floral designer. She has studied in England, done volunteer work in various countries, and lives in Tokyo with her family.

norikolivingstone.com